Living Life at 96

with Gratitude
for Grandchildren
and Beyond
E. Irene Theis

Living Life: At 96 with Gratitude for Grandchildren and Beyond

By E. Irene Theis

E. Irene Theis

Staples MN

Books by E. Irene Theis are all available on Amazon in Kindle and Paperback formats.

Art from photos by the Author's family, Pixabay, and Graphics Fairy

ISBN 9798835769391

Dedicated to my Grandchildren and Audrey Cassidy Carter, my Great Granddaughter

Contents

How God Answers Prayers

Sometimes when we pray and think that God has not answered our prayer, He is waiting to give us MORE than we asked for!

This happened to me AGAIN this week.

We were playing Bingo downstairs and my friend Marcella and her daughter were sitting next to me. I won two games and the rule is after two prizes, if we win again, we give our third prize to someone else.

So I wanted to win once more, just so I could give my prize to Marcella.

I was disappointed when I did not win again, as we went into Coverall. Coverall is the final game and the big prize and we are all allowed to accept that final, special gift!! I saw that Marcella liked the prize which was a beautiful Greeting she could hang on her door.

So what happened!!!!???
I won the Coverall!!!

1

Of course, I gave it to Marcella, just as God had intended.

Instead of a small prize, God answered my prayer with a big prize!!!!

Nina and Tina

Nina is very caring and helps all of us at the Manor whenever she can. She is 8 months pregnant but is still leading us in our Exercise Program at 10:15 am Monday through Saturday. Today when she found out that I was sorry I had not ordered dinner tonight since it was healthy and I was short on groceries this week, she spoke up and said she could still order dinner for me. There was still time and she would be happy to do so.

Tina comes to the Manor on Mondays and Wednesdays to provide special activities such as Bingo in the afternoon. She also is very thoughtful and helps anyone who doesn't hear or see well.

At 95, I do have problems, but it is important that I look for something each day to be GRATEFUL for.

I include Nina and Tina in this chapter
With Gratitude

Bedtime Stories by Irene

Since my bedroom radiator at my apartment at the Manor was waking me up during the night, and it was not fixable, Scott, Head of Maintenance, turned the radiator completely OFF. I had two choices now: the first choice was to leave my bedroom door open so the heat from the other radiators would come into my bedroom to keep me warm enough.

However, I sleep much better when it is DARK in my room. There is a light in the wall outside my handicapped bathroom next to my bedroom door so that I will not fall when up at night. When I leave my bedroom door open, the light shines in and I do not sleep as well as when it is dark.

My choice is between keeping warm through the night with my door SHUT or getting cold before morning but with a dark bedroom!

First Night

The first night I decided to try shutting my bedroom door. It was warm when I put my flannel pajamas on and went to bed about nine o'clock and since it was dark, I was able to keep warm and sleep well most of the night. However, about six o'clock when I needed to get up and go to the bathroom, I was shivering and I was cold and uncomfortable. I pulled up the extra blanket at the foot of my bed to help. Of course, I then opened my bedroom door and left it wide open
so my bedroom could warm up again.

Next Night

The next night I decided to see how it was with the bedroom door open all night so when I went to bed, I turned my head towards the inner wall trying to keep the light away from my shut eyes. Somehow my eyes still can tell when it's light or dark! It was much harder to get to sleep this way and I woke up oftener. I did not get cold and was comfortably warm all night.

However, I am going to try shutting the bedroom door again and experiment, as I read that it is healthier to sleep in a very dark room.

Special Sunday at Church of Christ

Thank you, God, for a blessed Sunday at Church of Christ with my dear family.

Cassidy and Ryan, my grandson, were here to celebrate their good news. How excited I was to hear that I would be having a great-grandchild in a few months. After the service, we sat at a table with Cassidy and Ryan for fellowship lunch and were soon joined by Pastor Barry and his wife who shared in Cassidy and Ryan's special joy.

I sat by Stacey and granddaughter Mandy and both helped me since I am still using my walker to ensure I won't fall. I remembered with nostalgia when Ryan and Aaron had visited me up north and we attended Malvik Church. Aaron sat on the piano bench with the pianist during the entire service and Ryan sat quietly with Grandpa and Grandma. After the service, the members remarked on how well behaved my grandsons were.

I was and AM very proud of my grandchildren.

How exciting to be having a great-grandchild!!

Churches I can Walk To

Last Sunday Dan checked out the Congregational Church next door and told me I could go there this morning at 9:30. When I arrived at 9:15, I enjoyed meeting Pastor Denise and a gentleman named Pat and talking to them. I gave Pastor Denise a copy of Living Life: Let Go and Let God. Then I sat down in the pew to wait for the service to start. Finally, about 9:45, the Pastor came to inform me that the service would be online for the next 4 weeks. She had not received the email.

I then decided to go a block down to the Methodist Church at 10:30 am. When I arrived there, I met a lady at the door who said the service was inside but on a screen since the Pastor was gone. She said the service would be on screen for the next 4 weeks.

When I met Tim downstairs, he again invited me to go with him to the Catholic Church nearby. He walks there every Sunday and loves it.

However, I decided to go home and watch on my Roku TV. I have a subscription there to watch Staples Church of Christ so that is what I did again this Sunday.

I have decided to talk to my son, Dan, about either going to Faith Lutheran Church or Staples Church of Christ the next four weeks.

Otherwise, I am grateful to be able to watch on Roku TV!

The Three Irene's at the Manor

The three Irene's exercise together mornings at 10:15 am Monday through Saturday. Here is a picture was taken before exercise class.

E. Irene, N. Irene, Irene M.

The three Irene's attend Chapel together
Tuesday afternoons at 4 pm.

The three Irene's often sit together for Ice
Cream Socials
And
For Sit and Share just to visit.

The
Tri-renes is the NEW name given to the three
Irene's!

Technology: Then and Now

To My Grandchildren:

It is almost impossible to believe the changes in technology from when I was 8 or 9 years old and now at the age of 96 plus!

Back then, there was NO television and NO computers. They were unheard of!
Back then, the phone was a wall phone on a line with others in your area. Each phone had a dial in number. You could listen on the line to other neighbors talking sometimes.

Comparing that to cell phone today is unbelievable! There is messaging, video's, face-to-face contact and more.

I thought of that this morning at 9:30 am when I was on my computer and dialed into a ZOOM call for Bible Study class. Advent Lutheran Church hosted the Zoom call from Maple Grove, in Minnesota, but there were also two members from Florida and me from Staples, Minnesota.

There were two views: one to see small pictures of each of us on the screen, and the other screen showing the speaker in a larger frame. Imagine: we could see each other as we spoke and we could hear each other as we spoke.

Sunday mornings when I cannot go out to church, I go on my Roku TV and sign on to the live Service at Staples Church of Christ which son Dan puts on U-Tube.

When I was a teenager, radio began. It was limited to sound, but we would go in the living room and turn on a show and listen.

Working for my son Richard, the owner and dentist of Elm Creek Dental, I became updated with finances on computer.

However, my grandchildren are WAY AHEAD of me when it comes to my cell phone. At 95, I think of it as a PHONE!!

Life Goes On

The last Sunday in February, I walked to the Methodist Church only one block away. I still had my walker but the snow on the sidewalk was cleared so I was doing fine until I reached the steps going UP to the church entrance. I asked a lady walking beside me if she could help me and she said she would help me with ALL the steps. I walked up the outside steps to the top, then she carried my walker up for me and gave it to me. We walked in the church and she helped me again with the inside flight of steps.
I realized later that she was the pianist.

 I saw Jacob inside who had helped me a few months ago and I sat in the back row with my walker right behind my seat.

They do not have a pastor now so Chaplain Paul Johnson came to preach the sermon and to give communion. I was so surprised that many people remembered me and greeted me. I forgot I had given someone a copy of my book but I was told she passed it around to other members and several told me they had read and enjoyed my book. In fact, one lady said she wanted me to autograph it for her sometime.

I can't remember names at my age, unfortunately, but one special lady was watching out for me and when I couldn't open my communion liquid, she came over and helped me!!! Then when it was over, she put on her coat, told Chaplain Paul she was taking me back to the Manor. She planned to walk the block with me but I assured her that after she helped me out to the sidewalk, I could walk alone OK.

I may continue to walk to Methodist Church the last Sunday of the month. I am so thankful to Pastor Elizabeth from Advent Lutheran Church in Maple Grove who assured me that whatever church in Staples I want to, Jesus would be there with me!

Thank you!

Let Go and Let God

LGLG Stories: Exercises

I just went down to exercise not really believing anyone else would be there since Irene S. was away. Usually it is just the three Irene's.

Kyle was working at the desk when I went by and as I greeted him my thought was that I would not stay since I knew Kyle did not REALLY enjoy leading the exercise process, but that he would do it anyway, of course.

As I approached the exercise place, there was Tim who once exercised with me but had not for several months. Kyle came to start the exercise and then Leonard came in to join us. Kyle led the three of us, Leonard, Tim and me and we did a good job. What fun!

Thank you, God, for taking care of life.

Let Go and Let God

Good things in My Life on March 14, 2022

Only about a week till spring when the snow will be almost gone so I can go walking outside again.
Daughter Debra came to see me last week and brought me a beautiful fish dinner, plus my Christmas gift from son Richard.
Debra brought me 2 rolls of quarters to wash my clothes.
I have a comfortable bed to sleep in every night.
I do exercises from 10:15 am to 10:30 am Monday through Saturday.
I had the booster shot for Covid 19

Yes, I still have problems to deal with.

I miss having my car to drive to church and to the store.

I miss visiting with my friends from Maple Grove, Advent Church and the writing group.

I miss working at Elm Creek Dental and training my grandson, Maxwell.

I would like more activities.

I miss going for long walks outside.

Life Gets Better

Sunday, March 27th, I again walked one block to the Methodist Church on the corner to hear Chaplain Paul Johnson again give the sermon and serve communion.

As I arrived very early, the same lady who helped me last time, greeted me at the front door and helped me up the stairs and to my seat where I could park my walker next to me. Later her granddaughter told me that her name was Joanne. Now I am determined to remember her name. I have a sister Jo Ann, pronounced the same, just spelled differently.

I was very surprised that I was not only greeted by so many but called by my name. A lady named Judie came by and told me she had my last book and reminded me that I had mentioned her name there.

The friendliness, of even the children, the message by Chaplain Paul, and the communion served were all God's Blessing to all in attendance.

Again, my friend Joanne helped me down the steps and out the church door to the sidewalk. I am not sure when I will go back as they do not have a regular pastor at this time. However, I feel most blessed and thankful to all.

Thank you, God.

Let Go and Let God

Elm Creek Dental Memories

As I near my 96th birthday, I am having memories of my past, mostly the good times that I enjoyed. Naturally most of these include my son's dental practice, Elm Creek Dental, where I spent many, many years. Some were when I lived up north and traveled back and forth about once a month.

Now I am missing living in Maple Grove and training my grandson, Maxwell, to reconcile the Elm Creek Dental bank statement every month, the simplest part of my work, but very important. I had learned over my many years of accounting and bookkeeping that bank reconciliations should be done by a family member rather than staff.

I was always thinking of what was best for Elm Creek Dental, which was only a TITLE as Richard, was the owner and only dentist. In that context, what was best for ECD included what was best for the employees, what was best for the patients, and what was best for Maple Grove.

All things work together for good!

MAY, 2022 a "WOW" Month

May started and ended with many unusual happenings, good and not so good!
First was the closing of the front entrance at the Manor while a new sidewalk was laid in front of the building. Everyone could only enter at the back door.

May 9th, I met Angie from the Staples Library and Dawn from the Staples World newspaper in the Chapel for 45 minutes. Angie brought my three books which would be placed in the library when the newspaper article came out. Dawn took many pictures of me holding up the front of the books. _Living Life: From Nine to Ninety; Living Life: Ninety and Beyond;_ and _Living Life: Let Go and Let God._

May 10th was the day I moved out of the Manor and into the Pines. I had been busy packing dishes, clothes and what I would take with me so that Dan and Stacey could move the small things first. Then Dan went back and met Pastor Barry, Gary and Tony who moved the large items, like my bed, computer, and other furniture.

The first week at the Pines was very interesting as we ate at large tables in the dining room and had many activities together. I met Darlene at my first meal. She saved me a seat and showed me what to do as it was very different than at the Manor. She also introduced me to several others at the table which she laughingly called the Faith Church table. I met Arlene Rice who showed me her published poem.

Unfortunately, on May 24th, because of several Covid cases in the building, all activities, including eating meals in the dining room, were cancelled. There was no bingo, no exercises, and meals had to be served in rooms only.

My 96th birthday on May 19, 2022 was simple, but thanks to my son Dan who took me to lunch in Staples. It was the only restaurant open at that hour but I had a very tasty lunch of my favorite, Eggs Benedict. There was a picture of me graduating from college at age 66 on the bulletin board and the poem I published about my younger brother, Donald Peter, who graduated from college and became the youngest full professor at the University of Minnesota. I received many birthday cards and also fresh flowers for my special birthday.

We are being tested every week and I am still negative. Thanks to God and a prayer for all Covid cases to be over in June!

Faith Lutheran Church

Taking the bus: Sunday June 5th

I was reminded last Saturday AGAIN to stop worrying and to LET GO AND LET GOD.

I didn't know if the bus would be coming to take us to Faith Church or if I should call Dan and ask him about Staples Church of Christ Church. Suddenly there was a knock on my door and Darlene was there to tell me that the bus was coming at 8:30 am Sunday morning to pick us up to go to Faith Lutheran Church.

I was so happy and immediately began getting my clothes and what I needed ready to go so I would be up and outside by 8:30 am, early for me since Faith Church is at 9 am. and Staples Church of Christ is at 10:30 so Dan picks me up at 10:15 am. I wrote out a check, checked the morning temperature and got my black light jacket out. I thought about where I would sit since I hoped to be able to go up front to take communion but had to take my walker which

29

was difficult depending on where I was sitting. I went to bed early with everything ready to go.

Sunday morning I was ready early and walked out to the front early to find Darlene and Jo Ann also ready to go. At 8:30 the bus arrived and the driver helped me get aboard and put my walker on with me. We waited for several others to come out and board. Then I was surprised to see how many other stops we made, including picking up my friend, Enid, at the Manor where I lived until May 10th when I moved to the Pines.

It was the Day of Pentecost and a special church service. I decided to have my communion delivered to my seat instead of trying to take my walker up front for communion. Enid, Darlene and I were served communion together.

Another pleasant surprise, after the service, strawberry shortcake was served in the dining room. While eating shortcake and drinking coffee, I enjoyed meeting and talking so some nice people for nearly an hour before taking the bus back to the Pines. We actually drove past my son's home where my car was parked in the driveway.

**Thank you to God for this very special Sunday
Service, Communion, and Fellowship.
I need to always remember to
LET GO AND LET GOD!**

Great Granddaughter

In my last book I wrote about the wedding of my grandson Ryan and his wife, Cassidy, in Pella, Iowa. Now I want to share the birth of their daughter Audrey. They drove from Hugo, Minnesota to Staples and brought their beautiful daughter to church at Staples Church of Christ on Sunday.

Monday, Dan, Mandy, Ryan and Cassidy brought Audrey to the back yard of the Pines. We went to the Cabana so that I could sit down and hold Audrey In my arms. She was so responsive when I talked to her and rocked her. She smiled and cooed. When she became hungry and heard her mother's voice, she had an accepting look, well aware of her mother's voice. What a joy to spend this time together!

Audrey Cassidy Carter

About the Author

L ET ME INTRODUCE MYSELF --

My name is Irene Theis. I am 96 years young and next year I plan on being 95 years young. I graduated from Metropolitan State University in Minnesota when I was 66 years old.

I am a personal testimony that the aging process can be reversed. In my former life, I was an Executive and Trainer with a large financial in the Twin Cities Area. Unfortunately, it was a Savings and Loan, and most of you know what happened a few years ago to that industry. Many of us lost our pensions and health benefits at that time. However, I believe "all things work together for good", and despite the hardships at that time, I started my own business and am now doing what I love doing—helping others by showing them how to achieve both health and wealth. I have always been concerned with health issues.

As a member of Business and Professional Women (BPW), I was interested in women's issues, especially women's health, and yes, in their economic status. I became involved, attended seminars, workshops, and researched both the health and financial problems of women. After retirement, I didn't want to live in a nursing home, incapacitated, and dead broke! I wanted to live to be old in a youthful state. That is still my goal.

Email: evairene19@gmail.com

Other Titles by E. Irene Theis

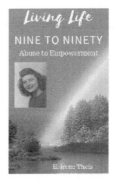

Living Life: From Nine to Ninety;

Living Life: Ninety and Beyond

Living Life: Let Go and Let God

Made in the USA
Middletown, DE
18 June 2022